GERMANY AND SWITZERLAND

PHOTOGRAPHS BY ELIZABETH KRAMER

THIS IS PART OF THE VISITING SERIES.

GERMANY (MUNICH & BAVARIA)

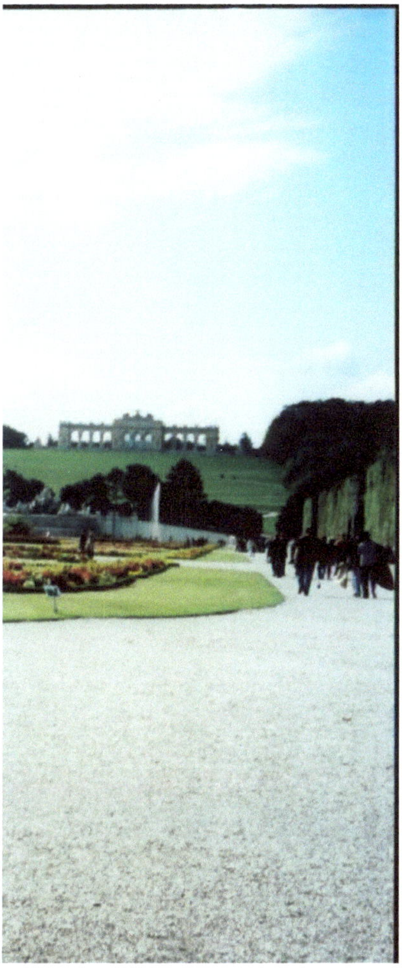

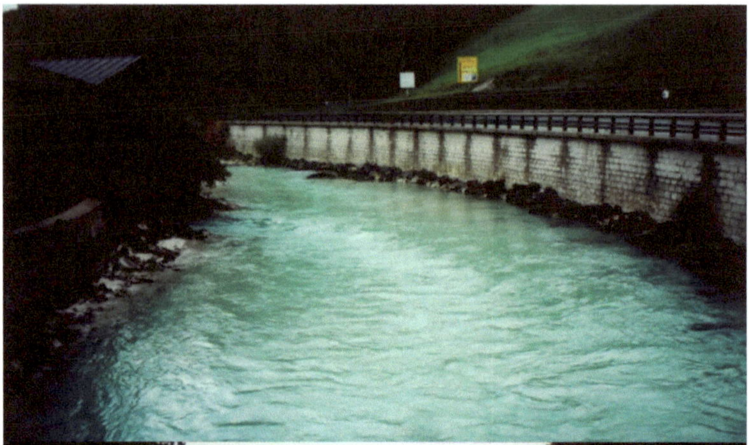

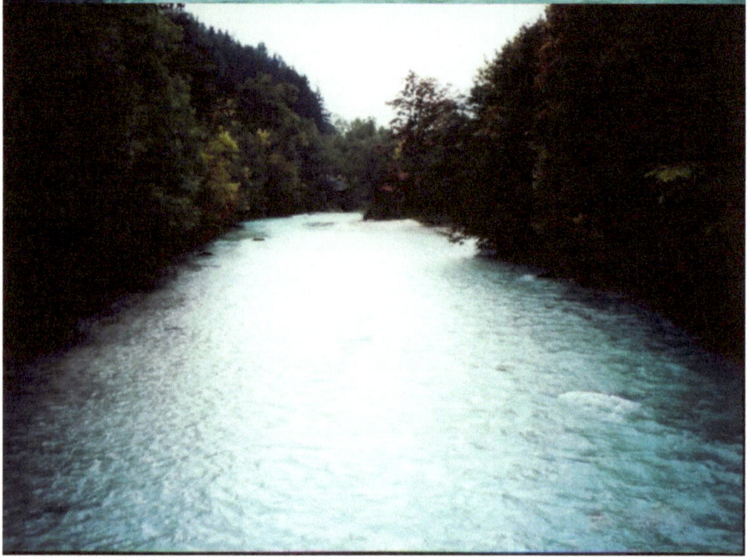

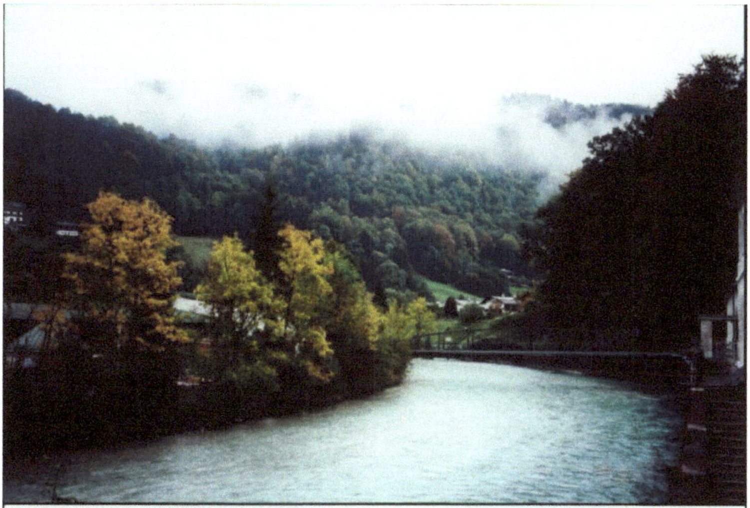

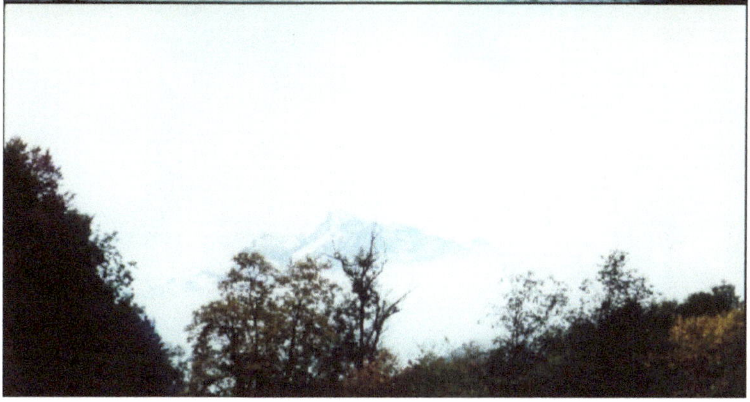

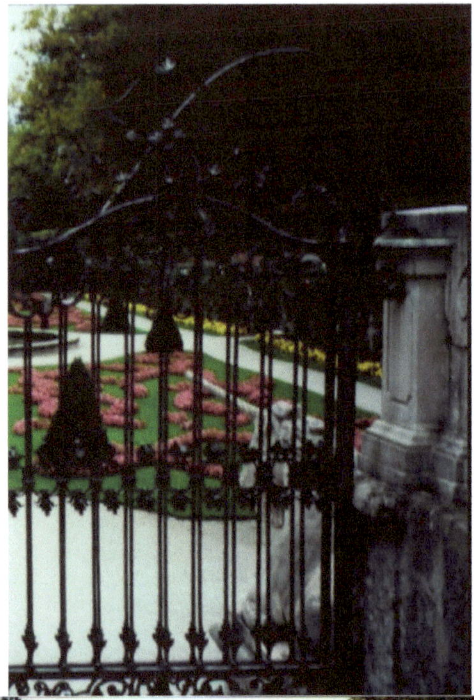

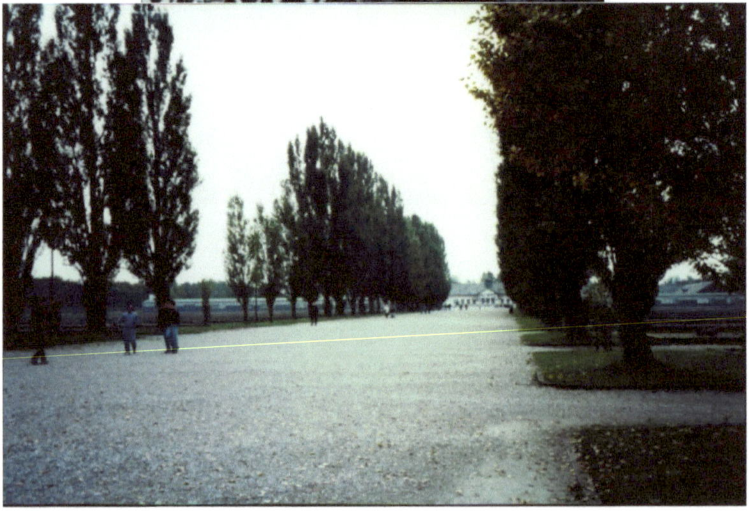

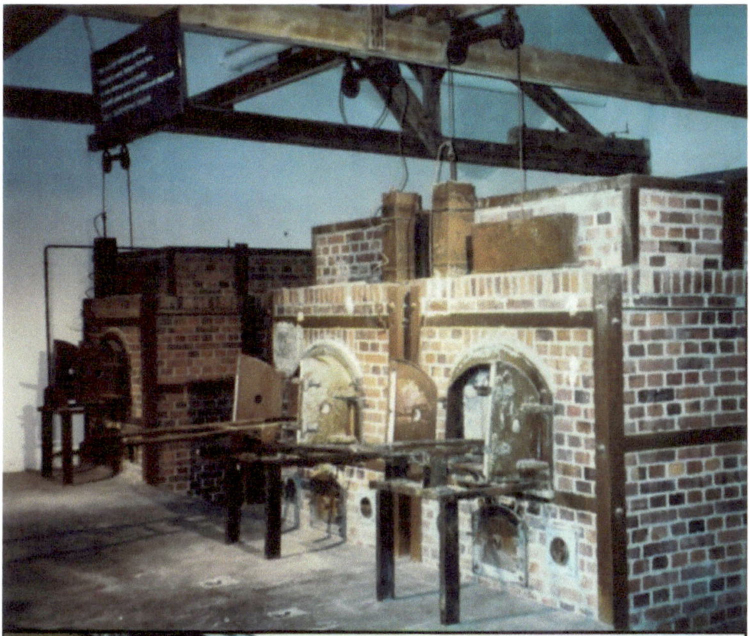

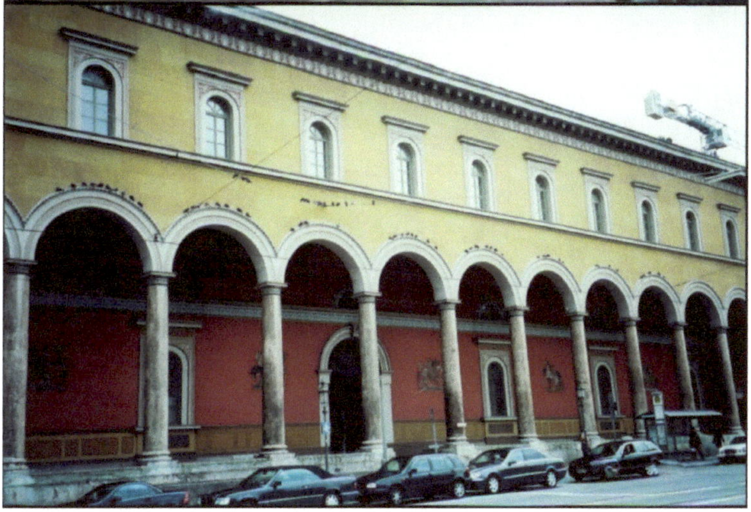

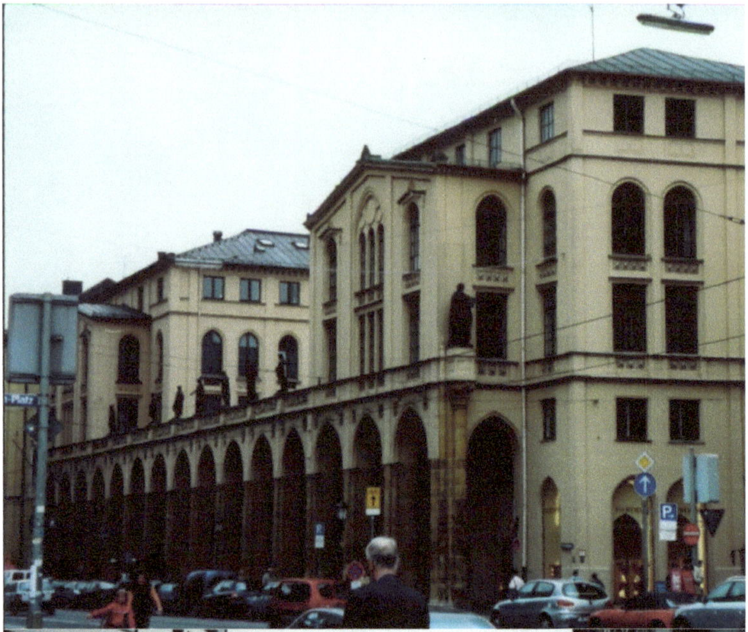

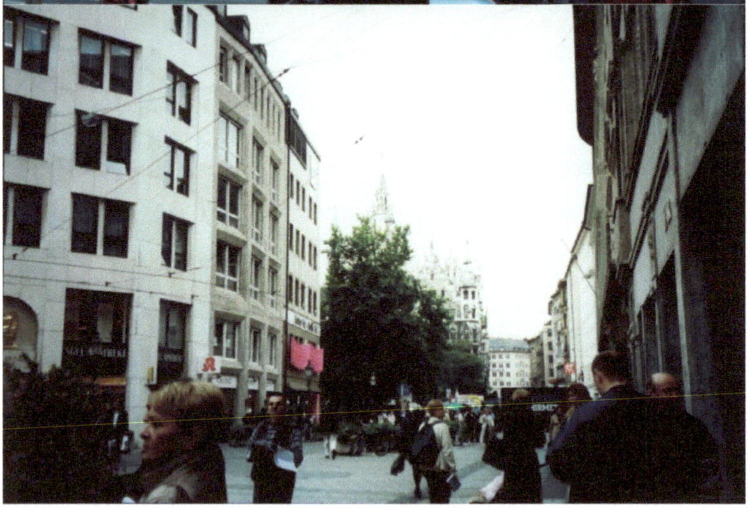

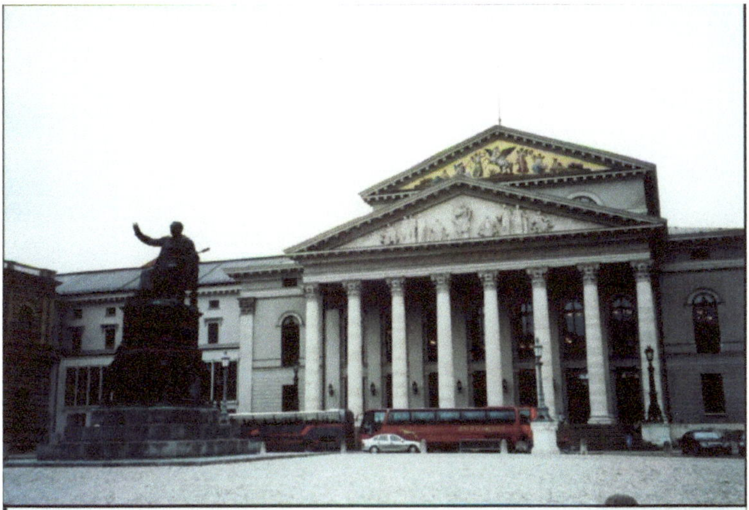

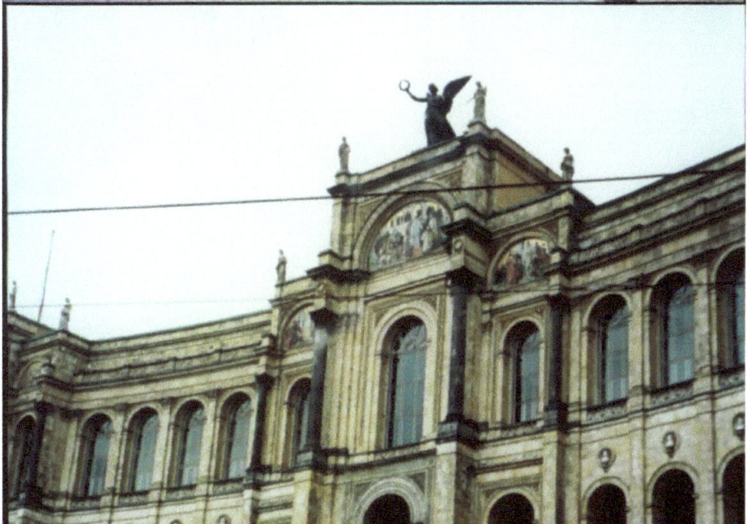

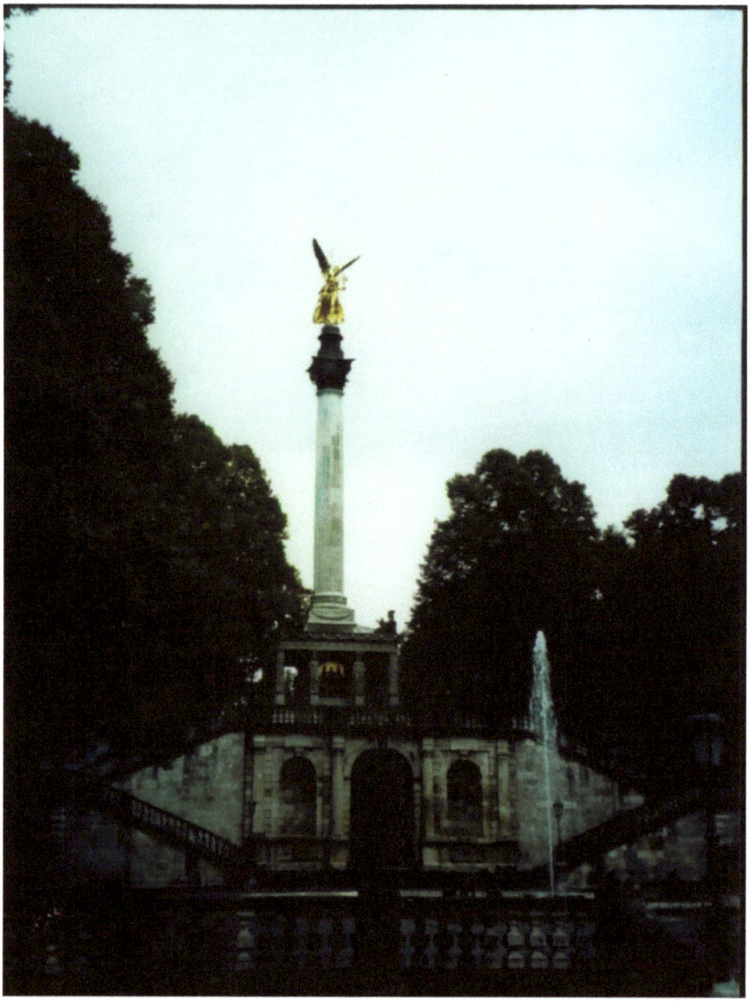

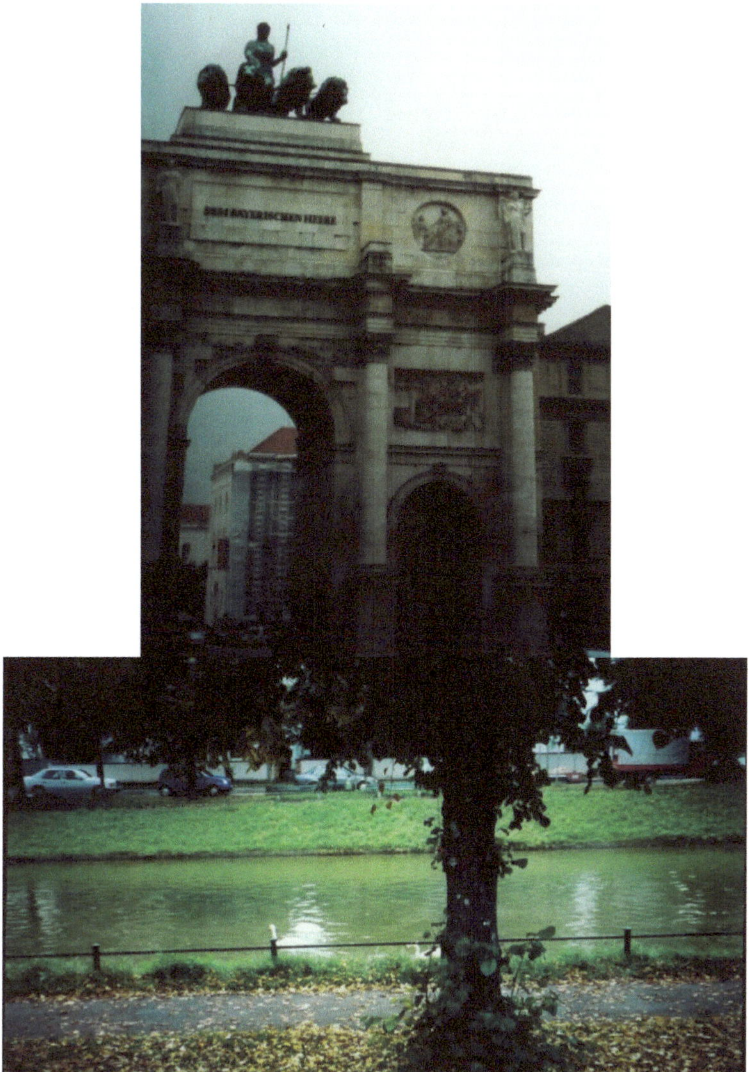

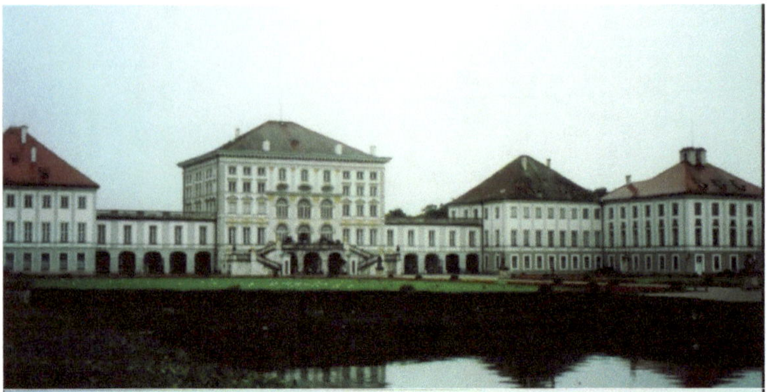

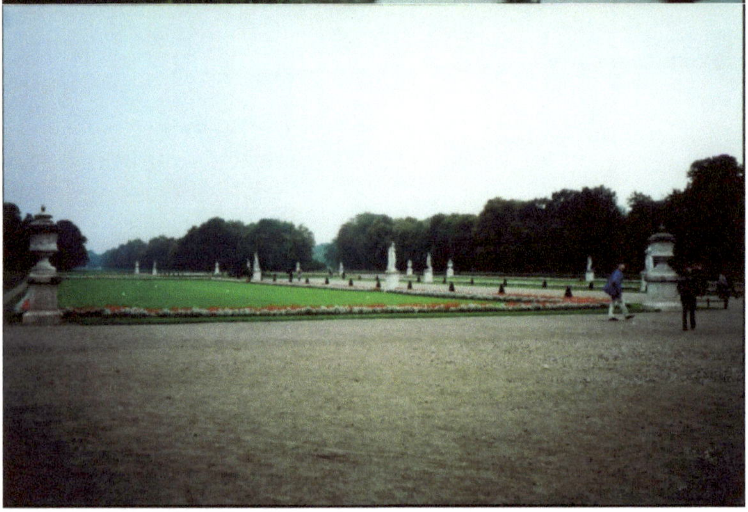

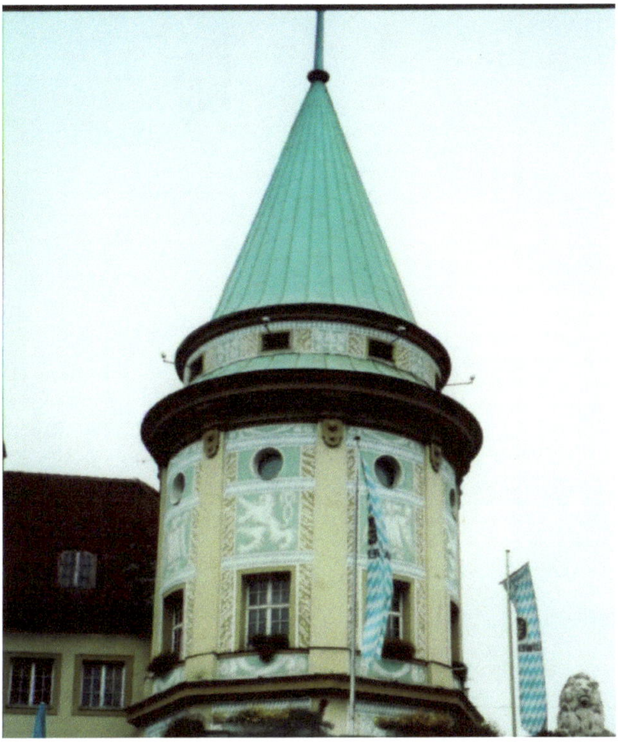

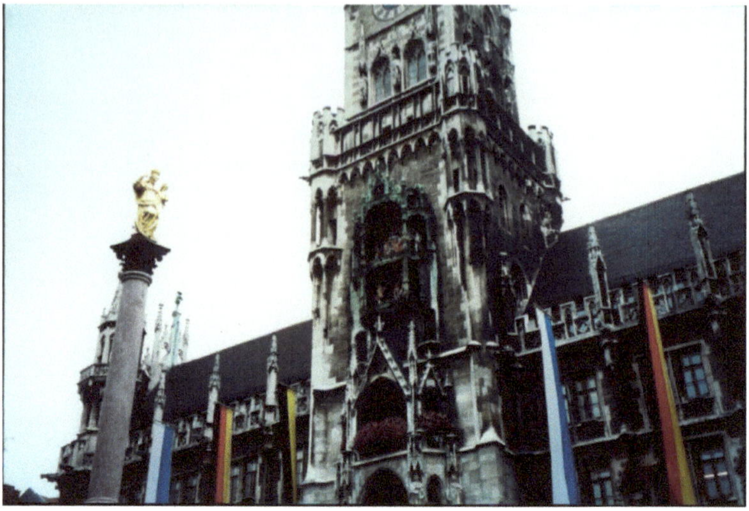

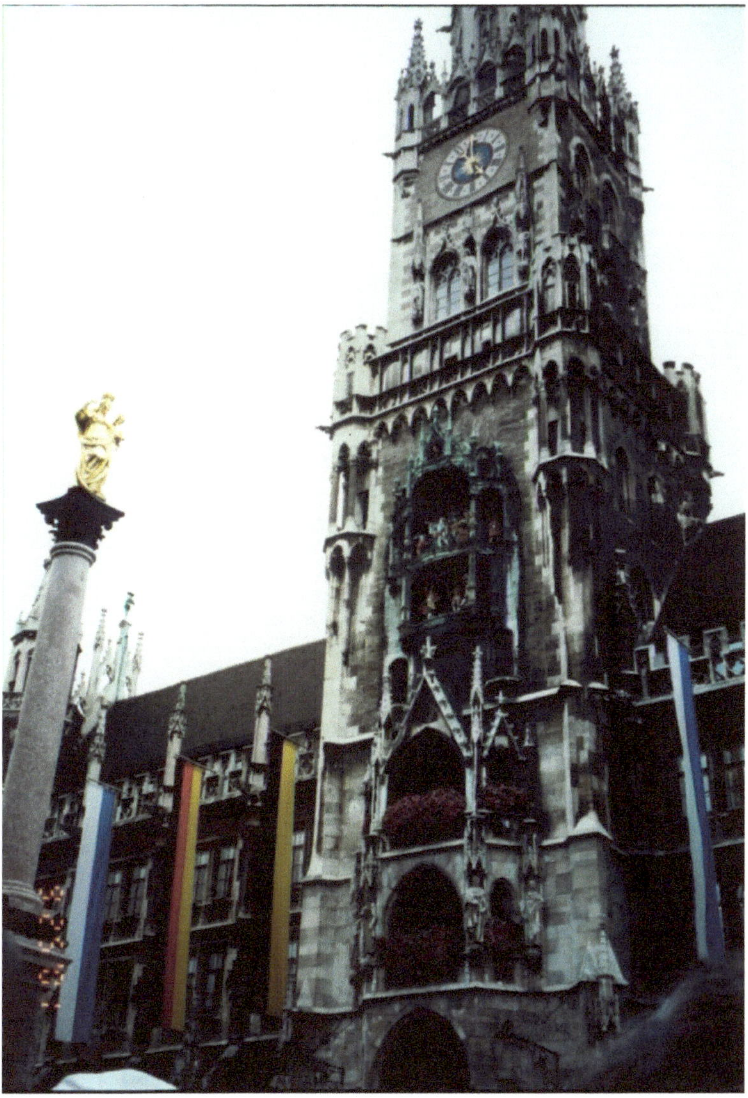

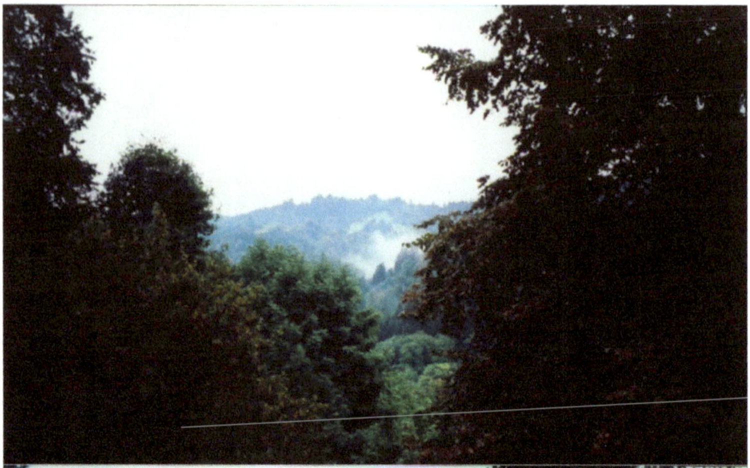

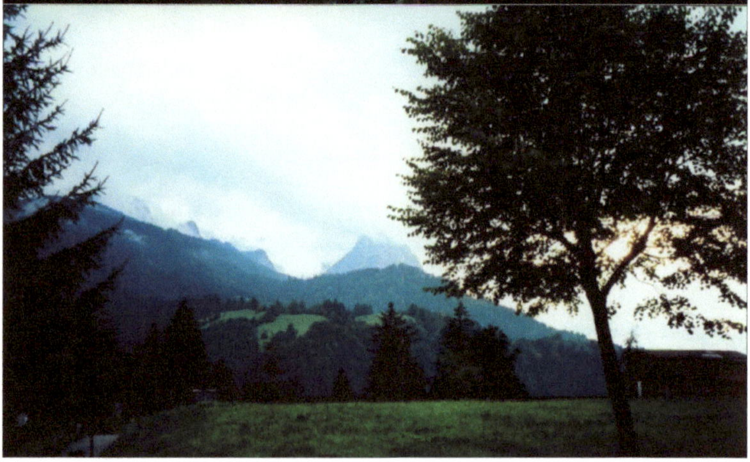

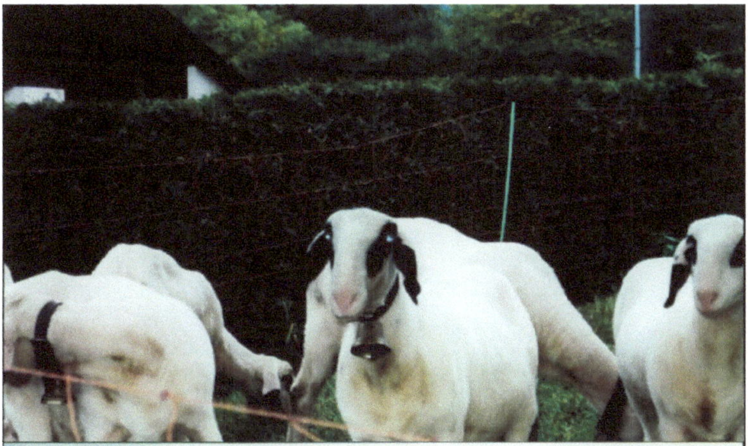

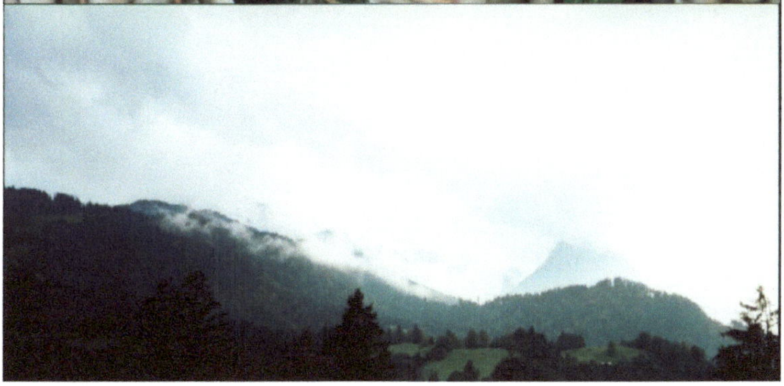

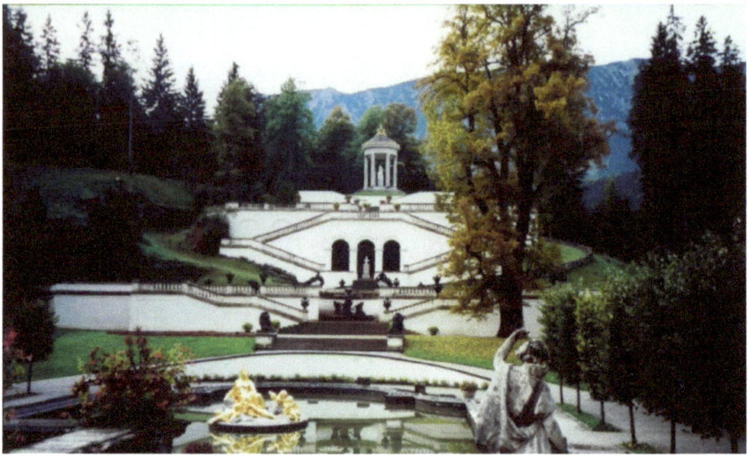

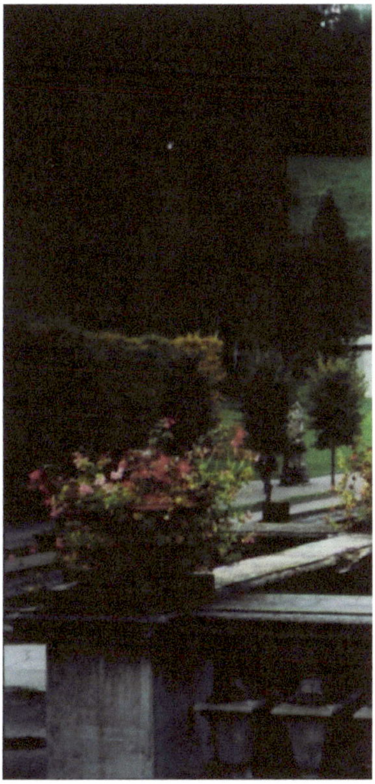

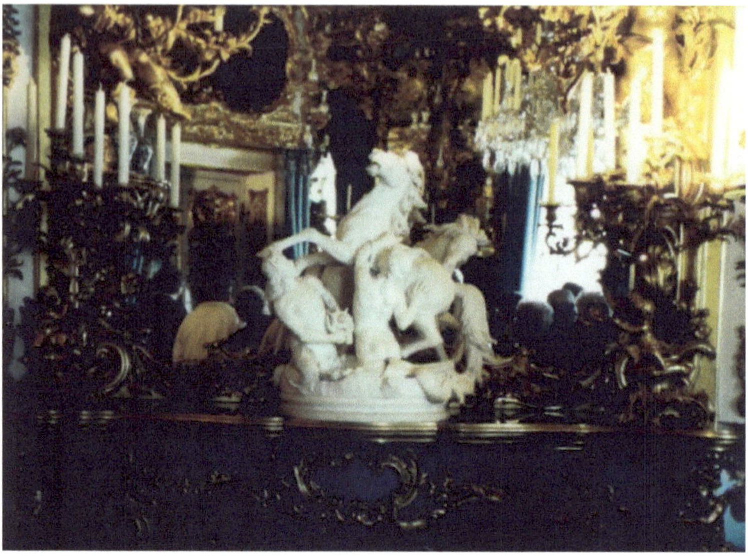

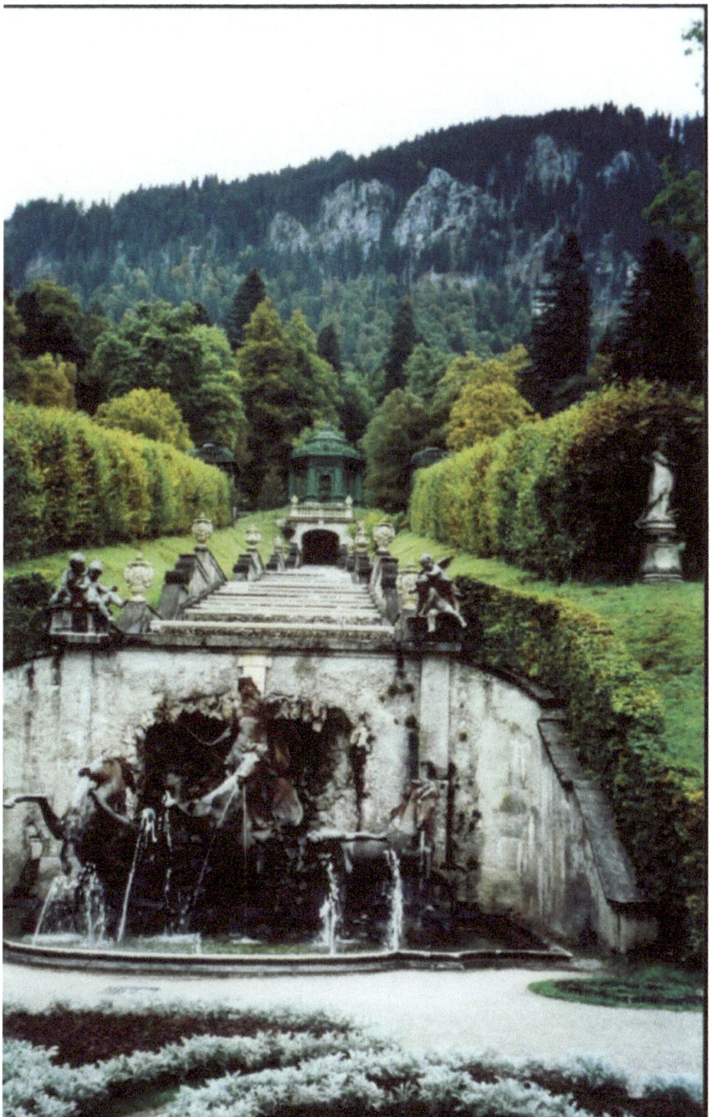

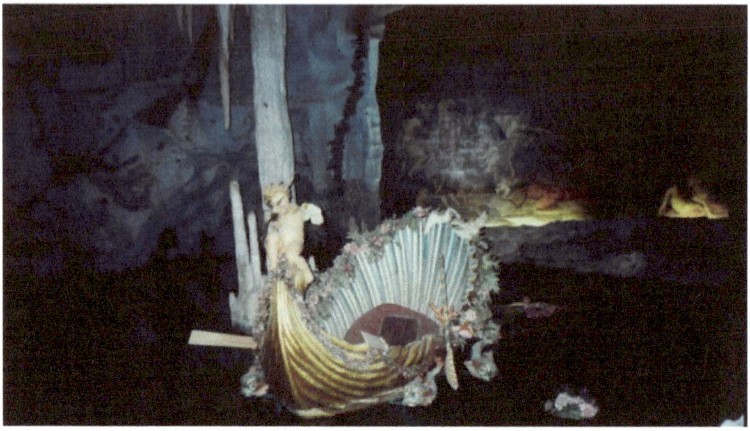

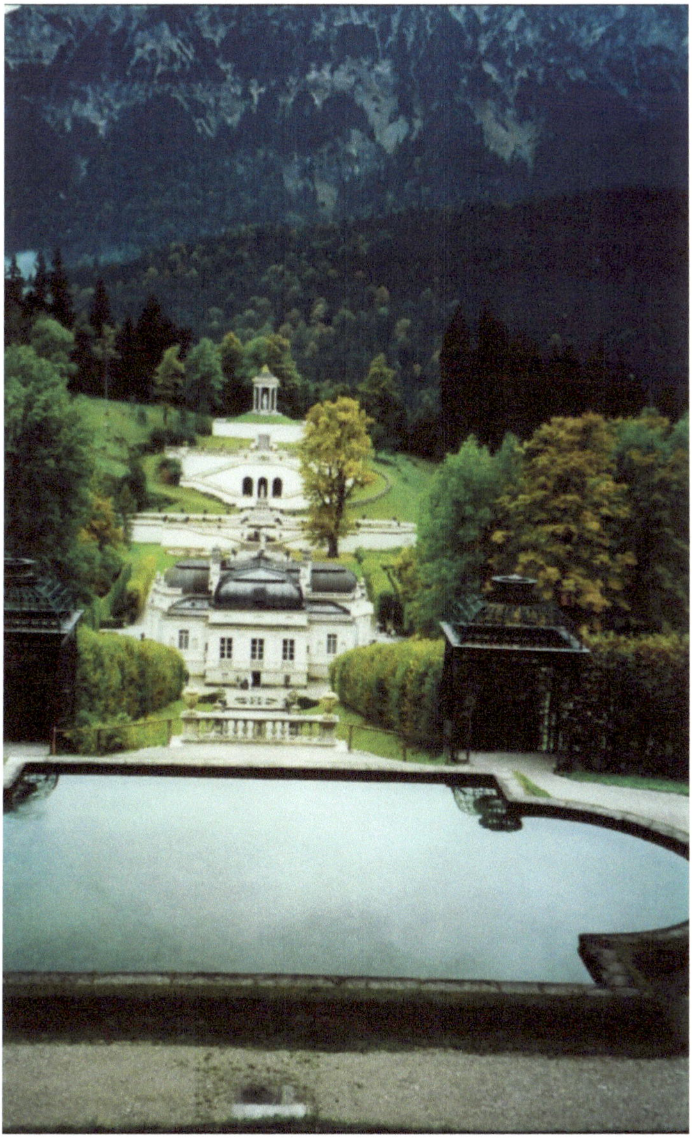

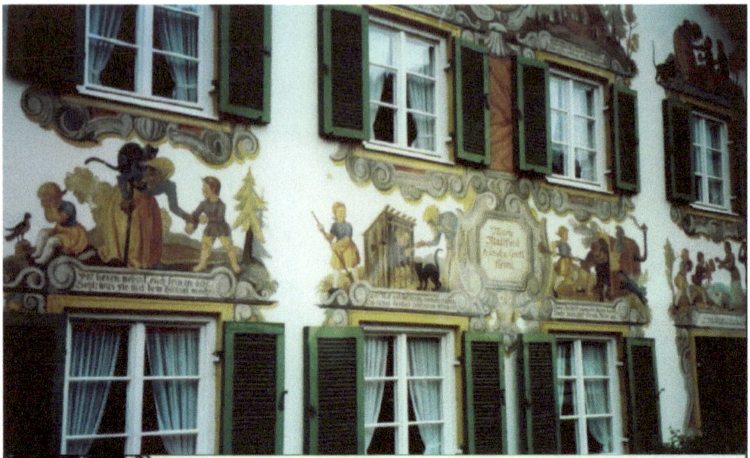

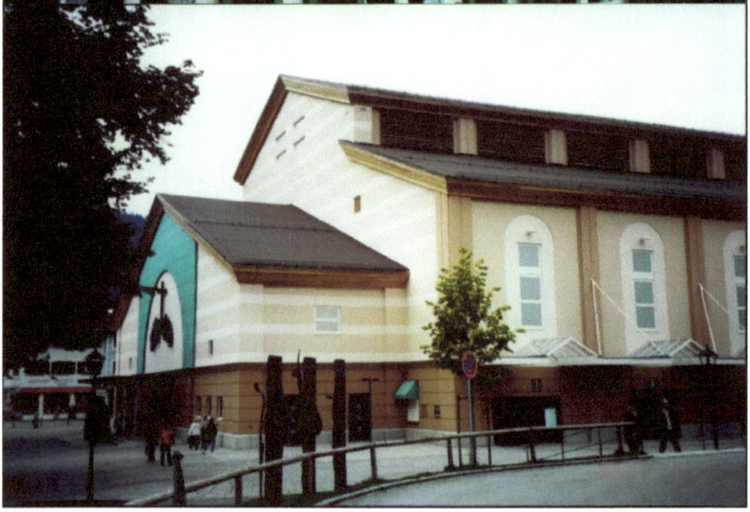

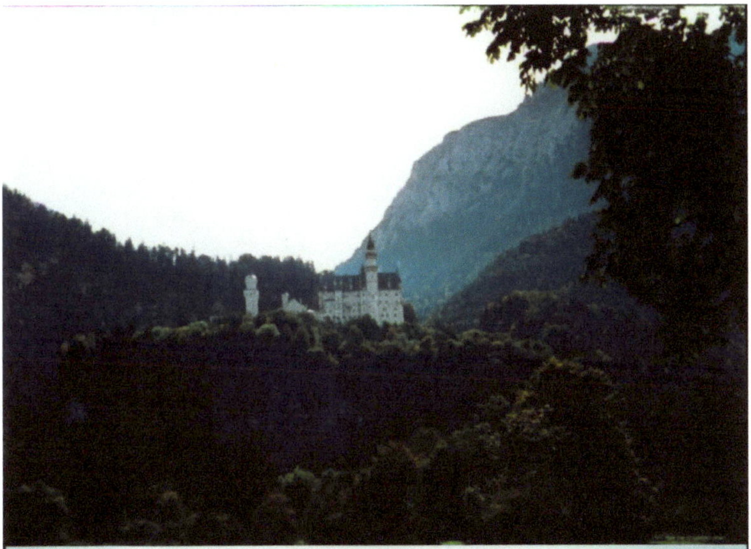

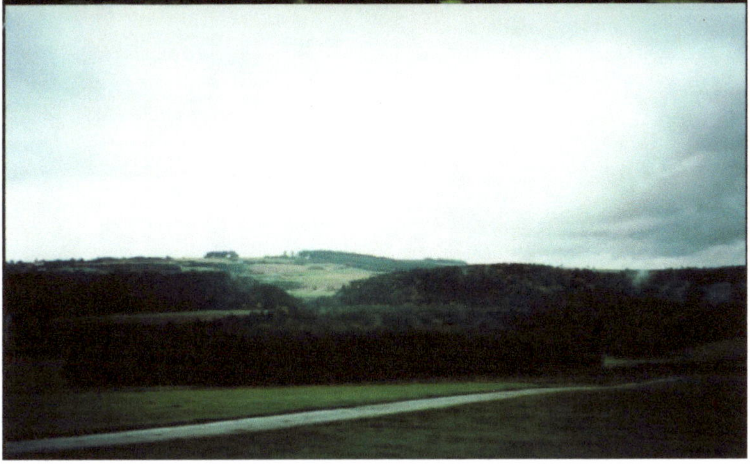

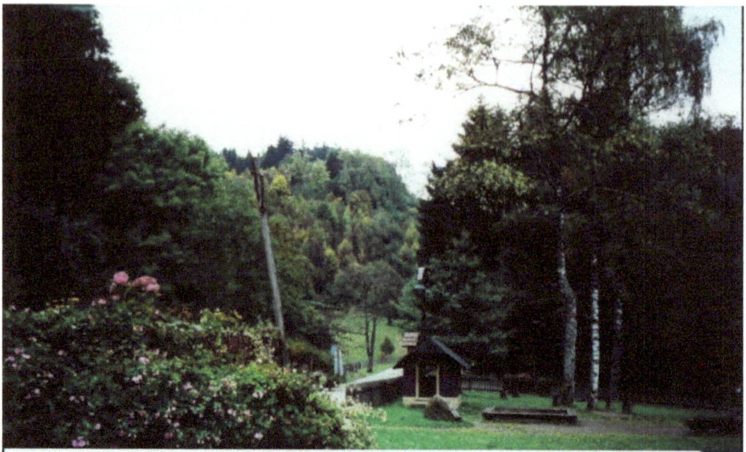
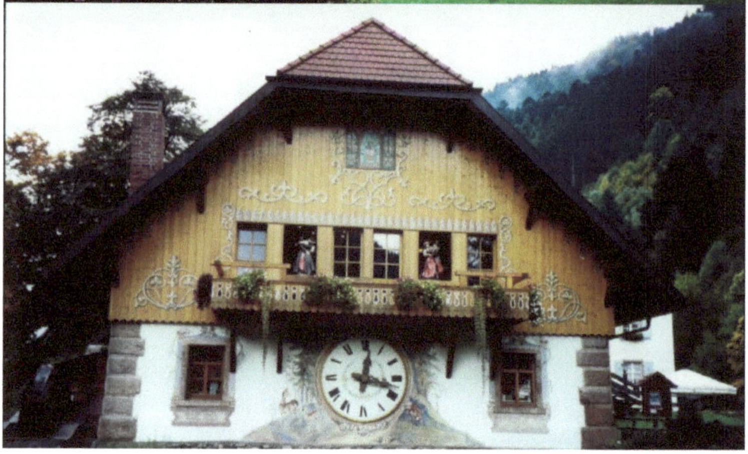

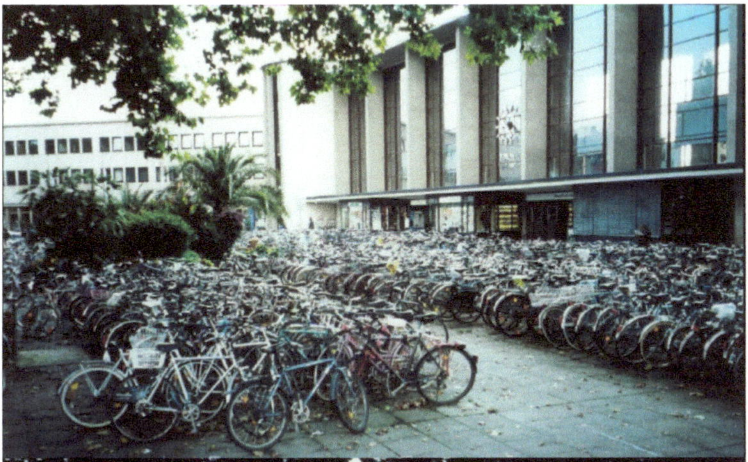

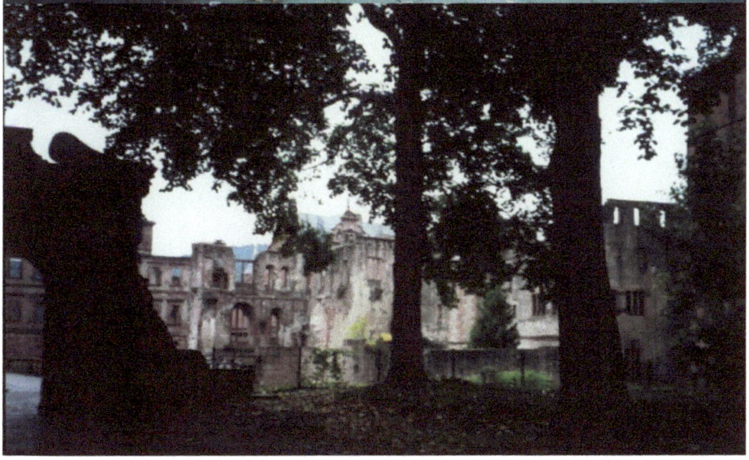

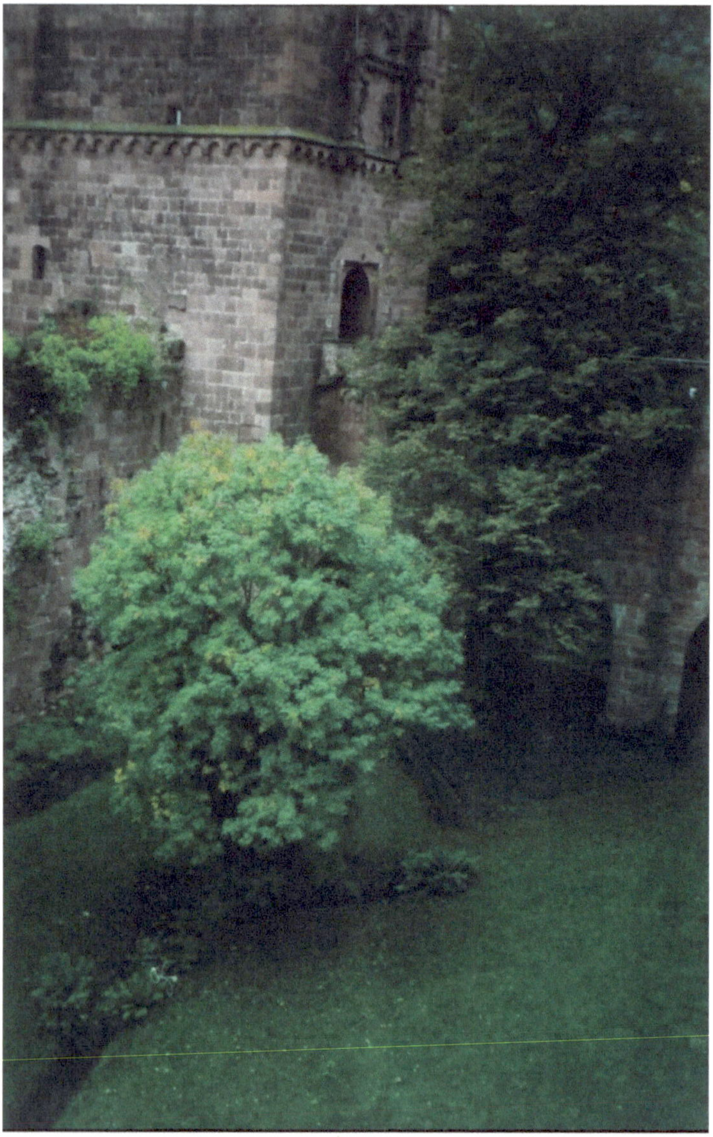

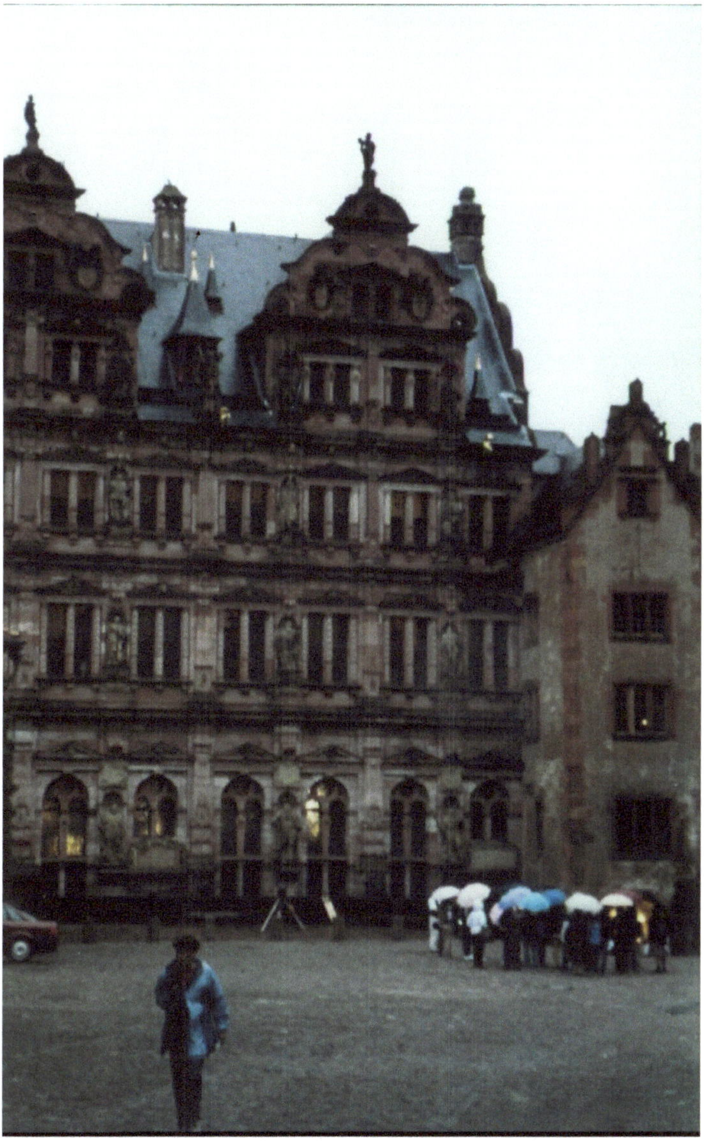

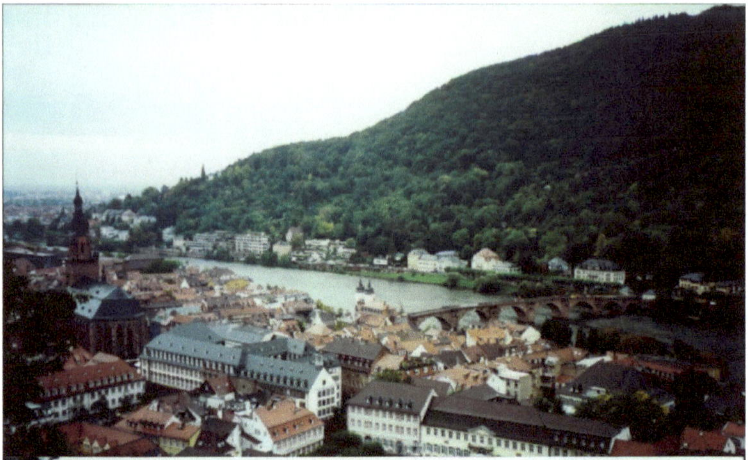

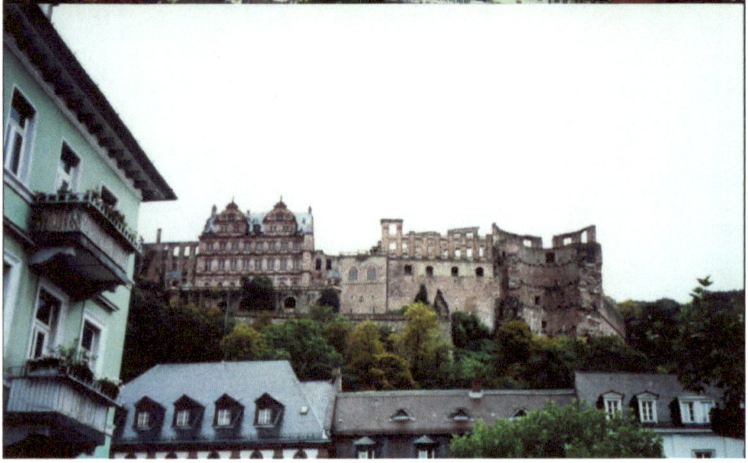

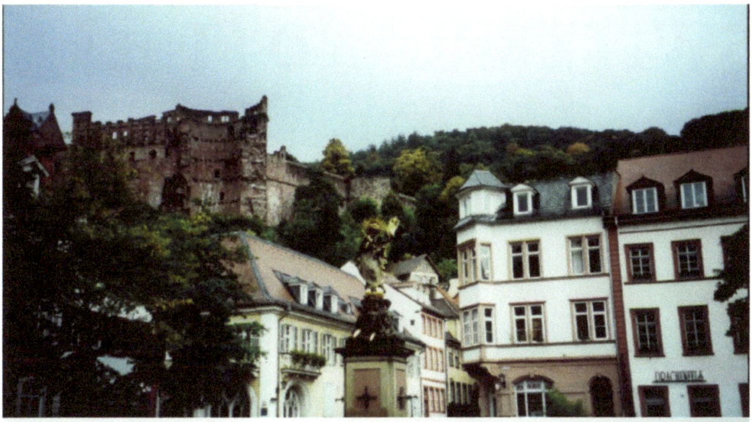

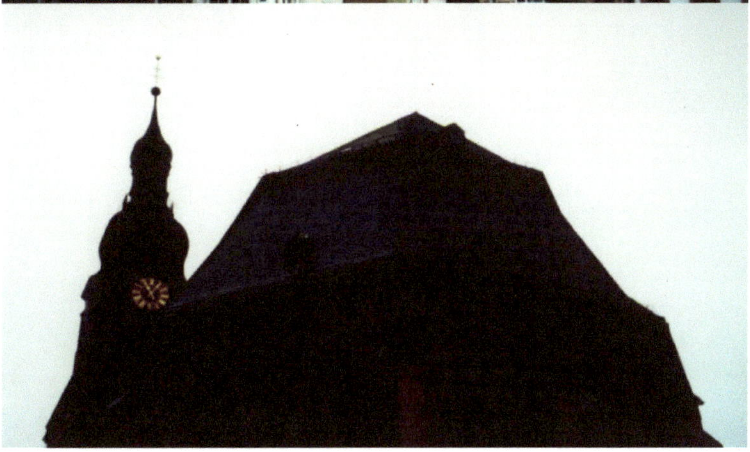

SWITZERLAND (THE ALPS, LIECHTENSTEIN & LUCERNE)

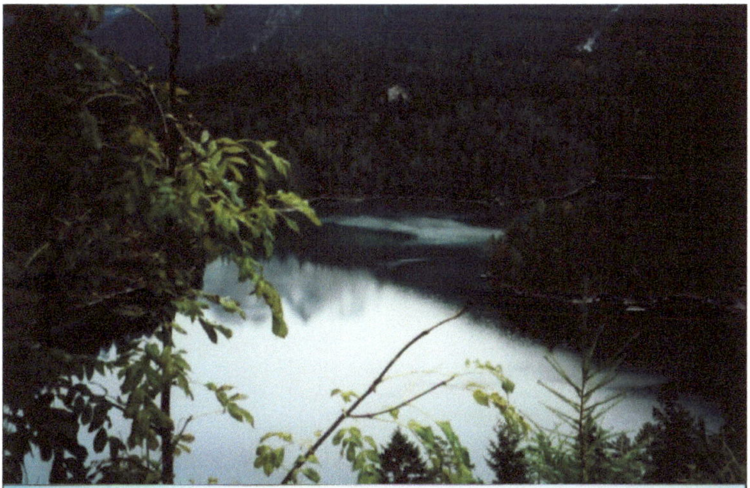

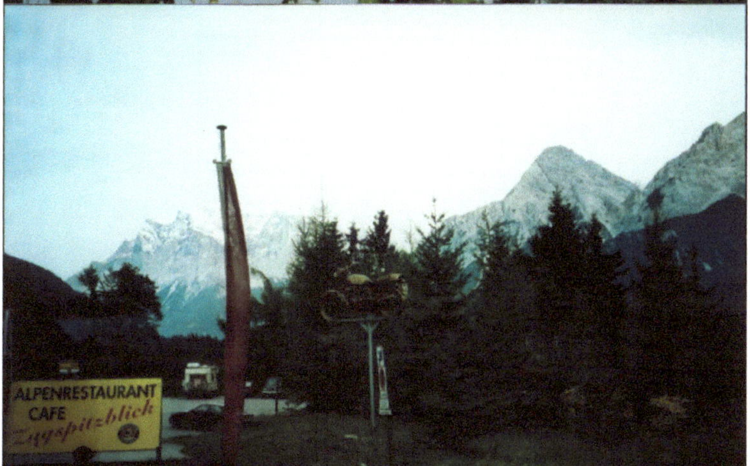
ALPENRESTAURANT
CAFE
Zugspitzblick

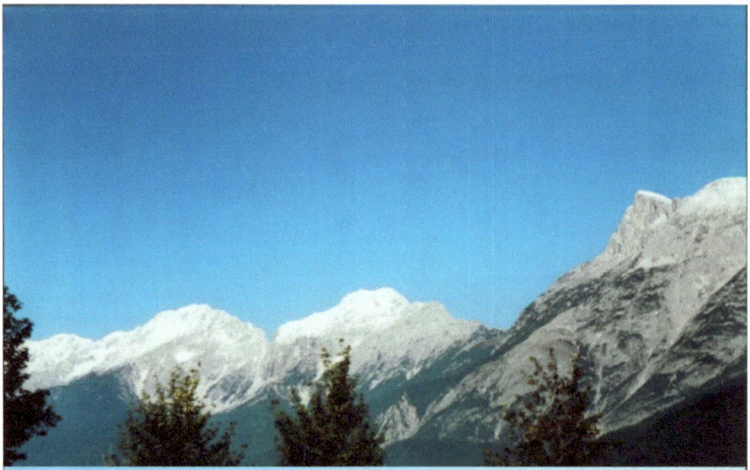

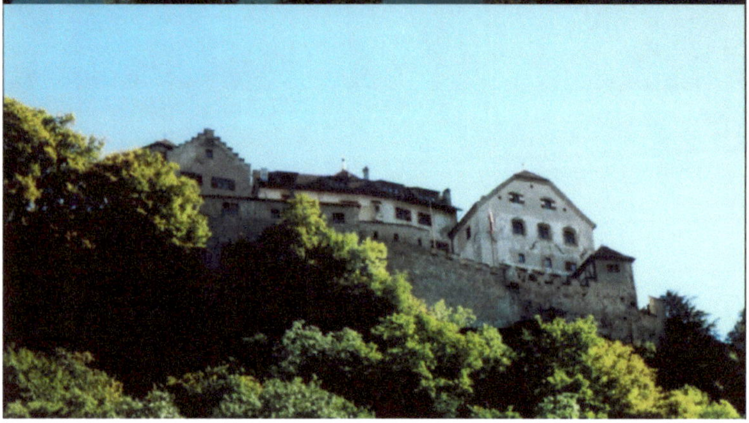

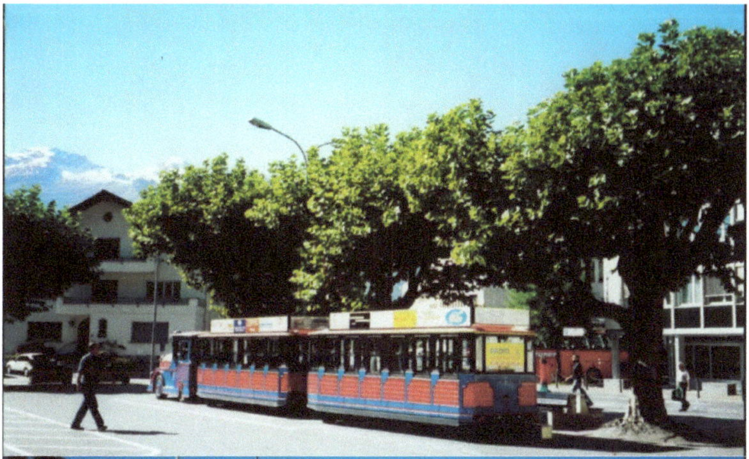

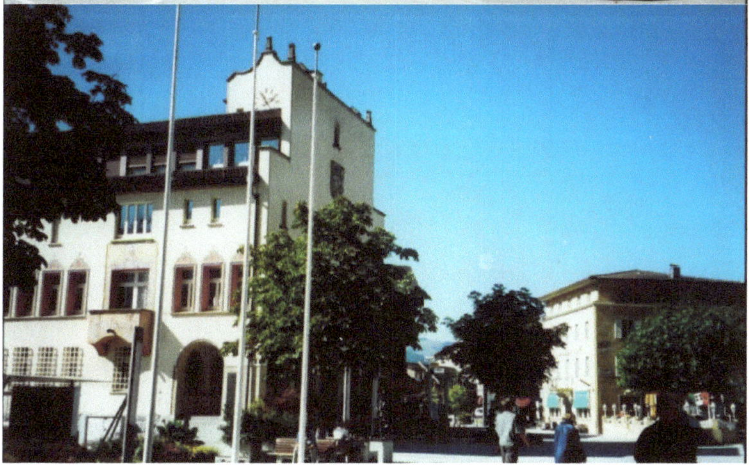

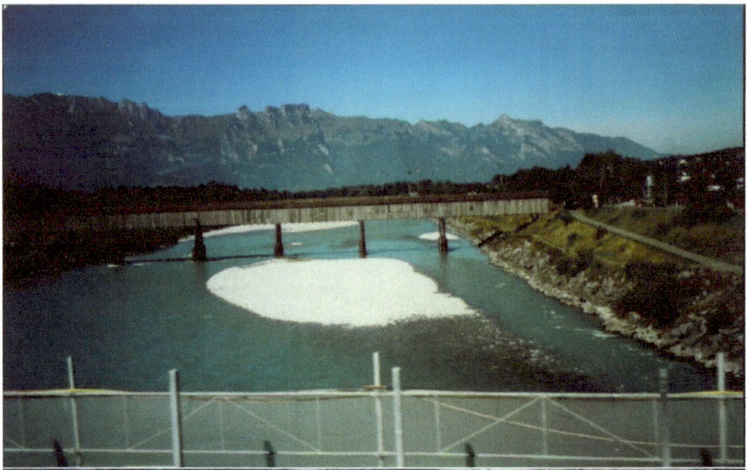

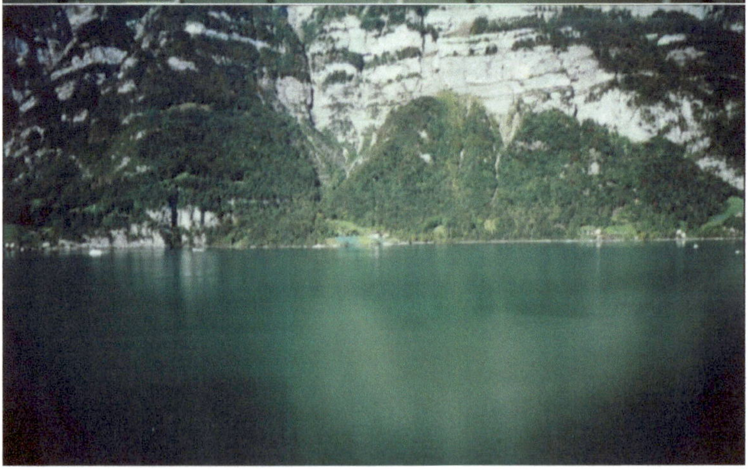

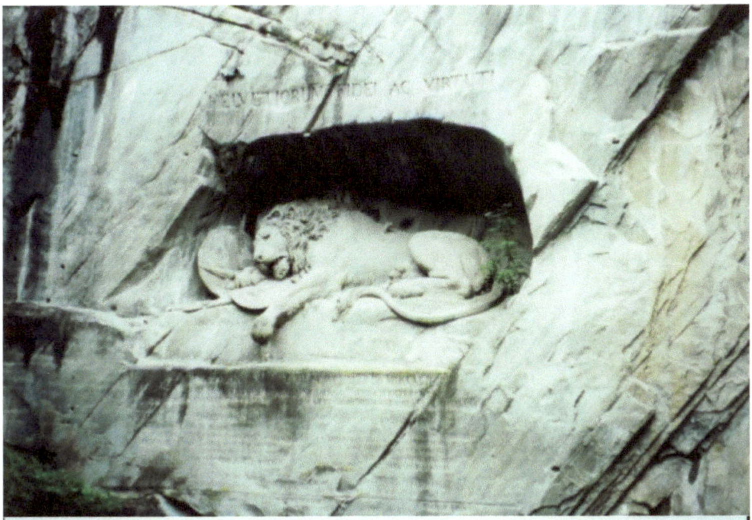

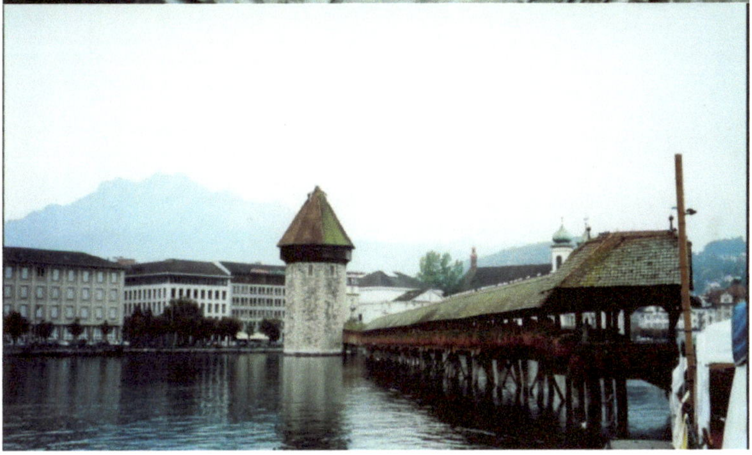

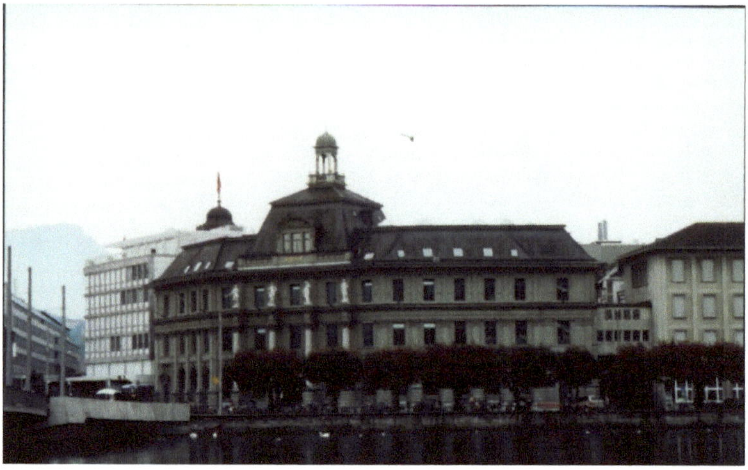

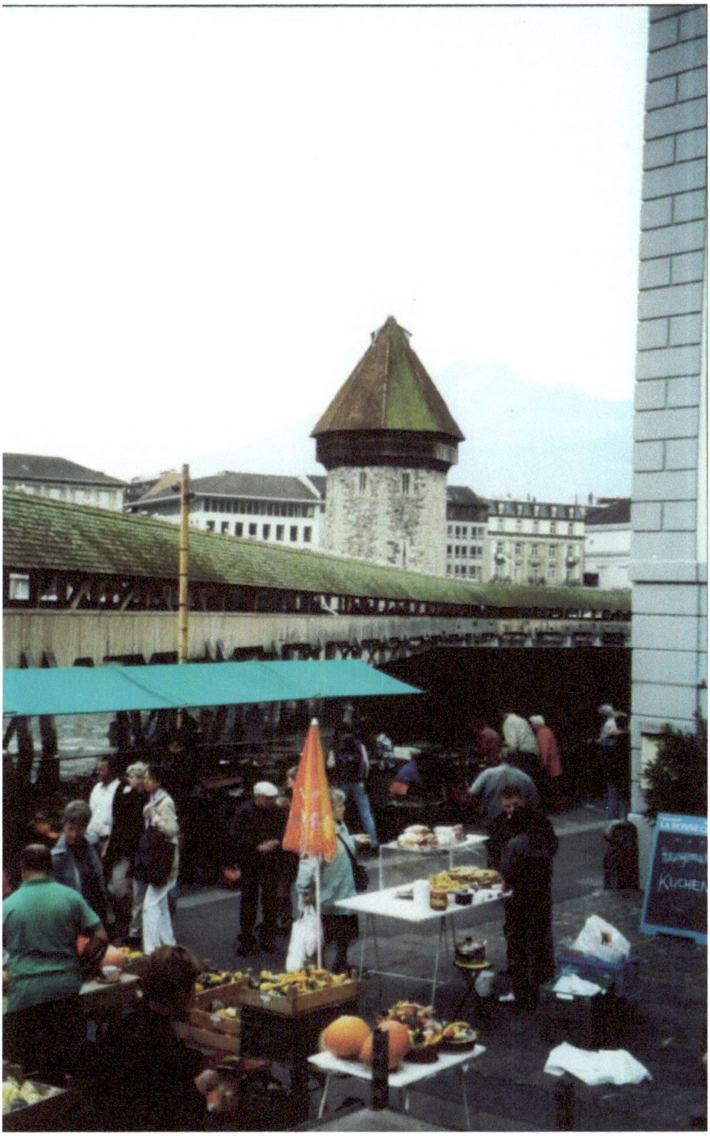

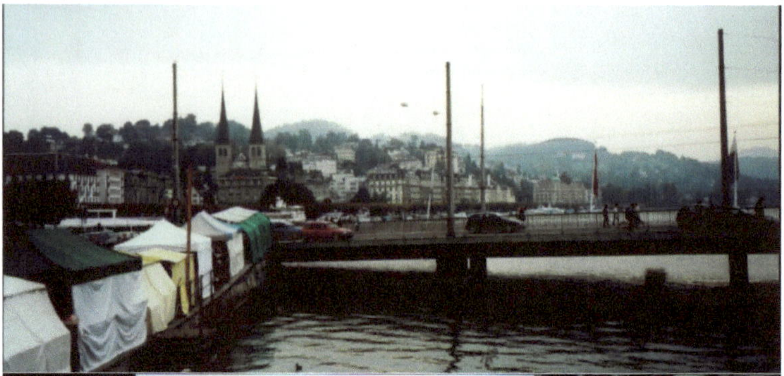

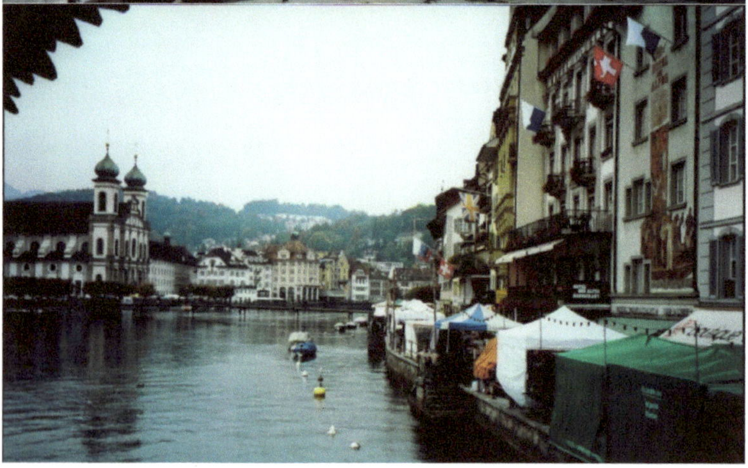

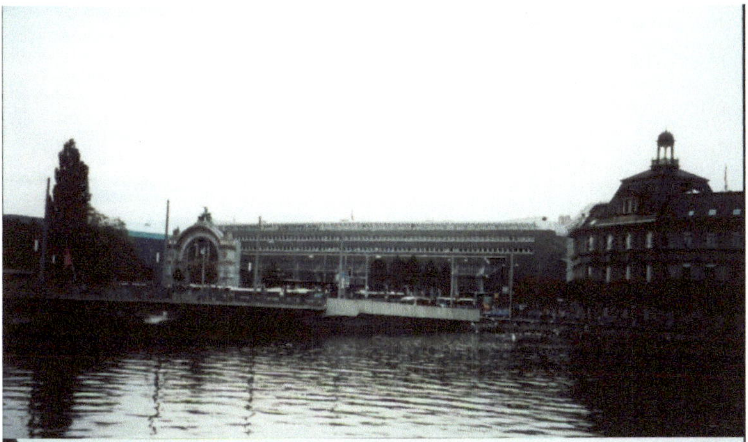

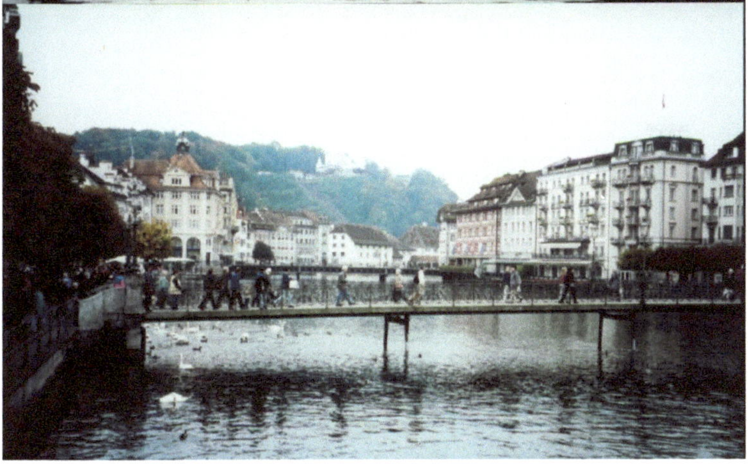

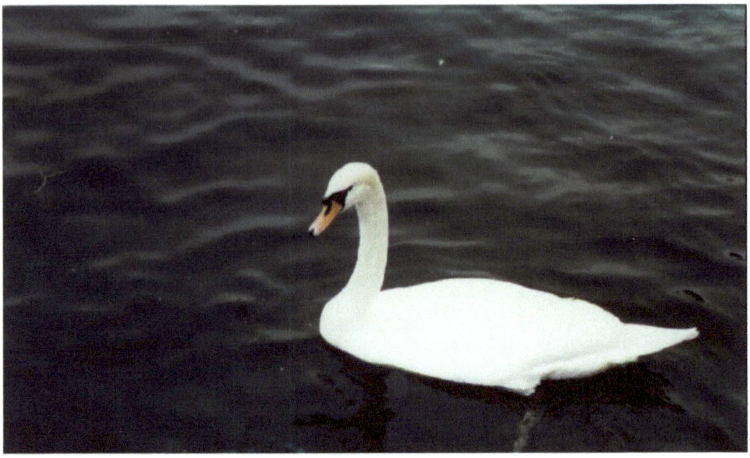

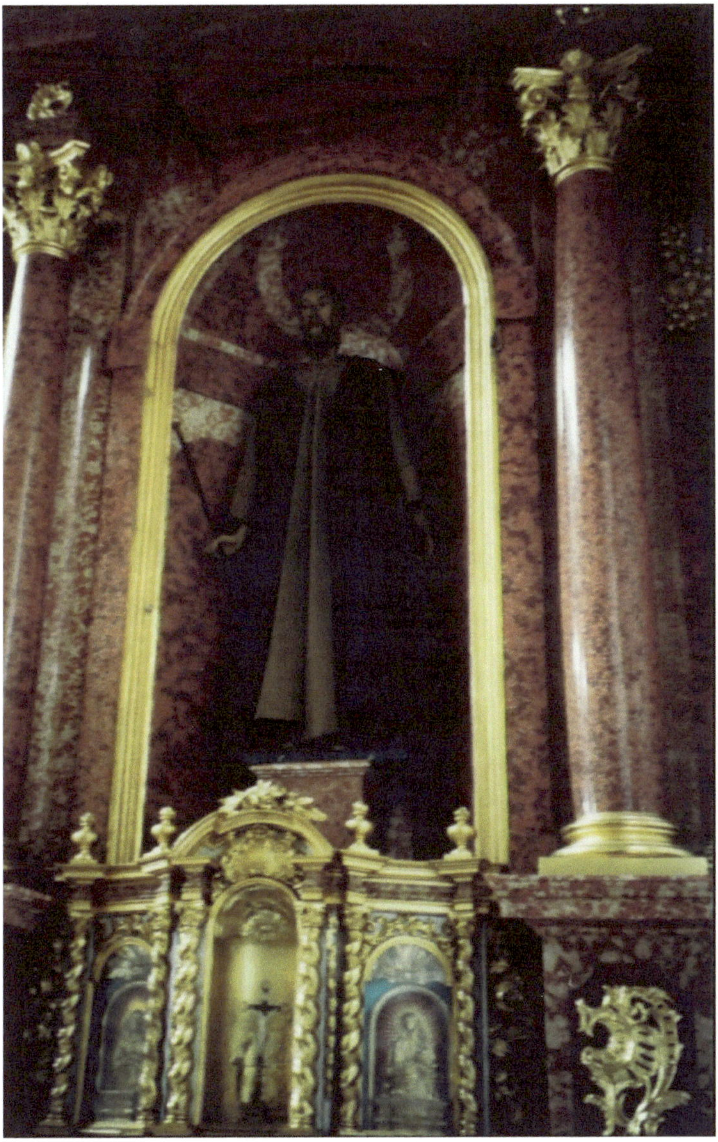

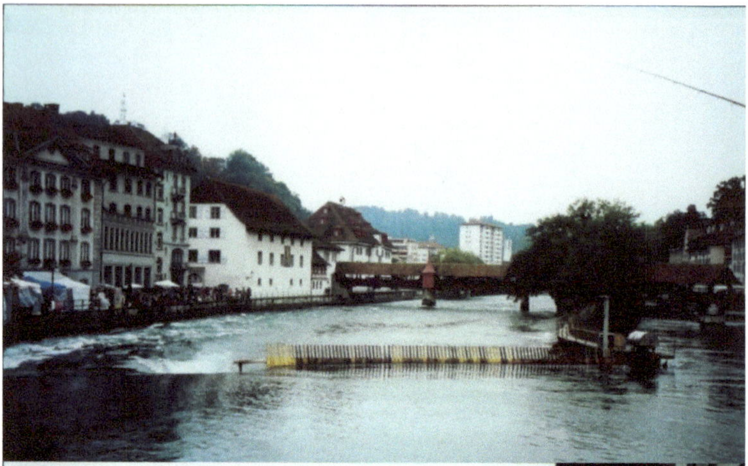

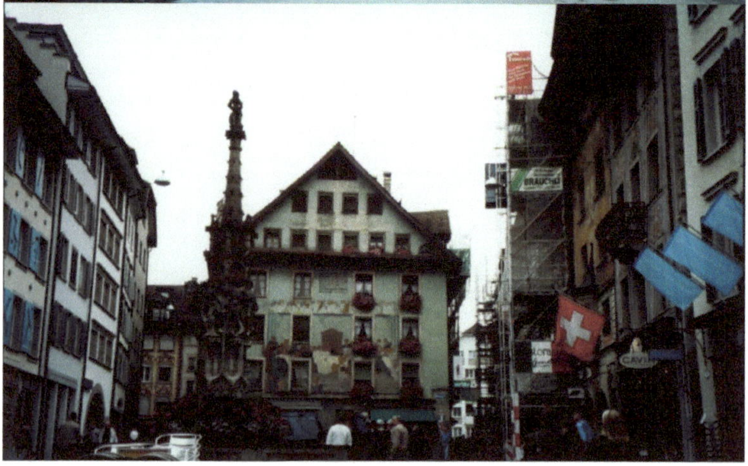

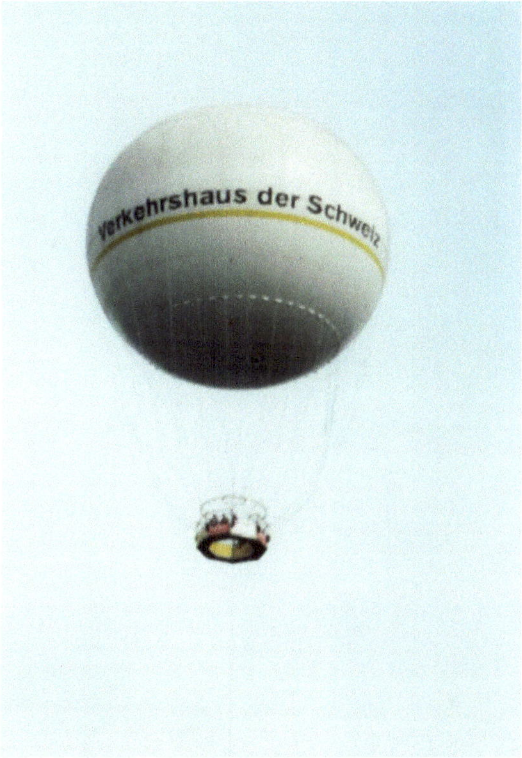
Verkehrshaus der Schweiz

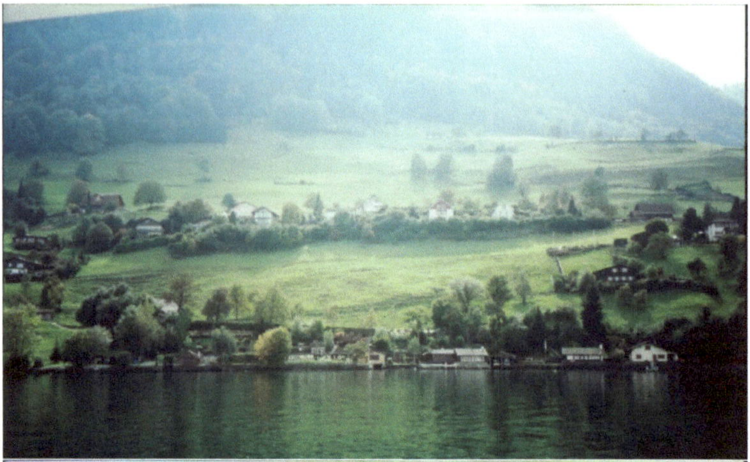

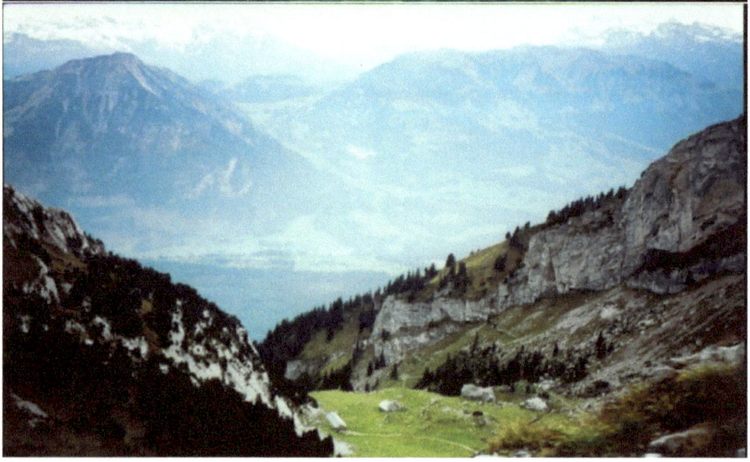

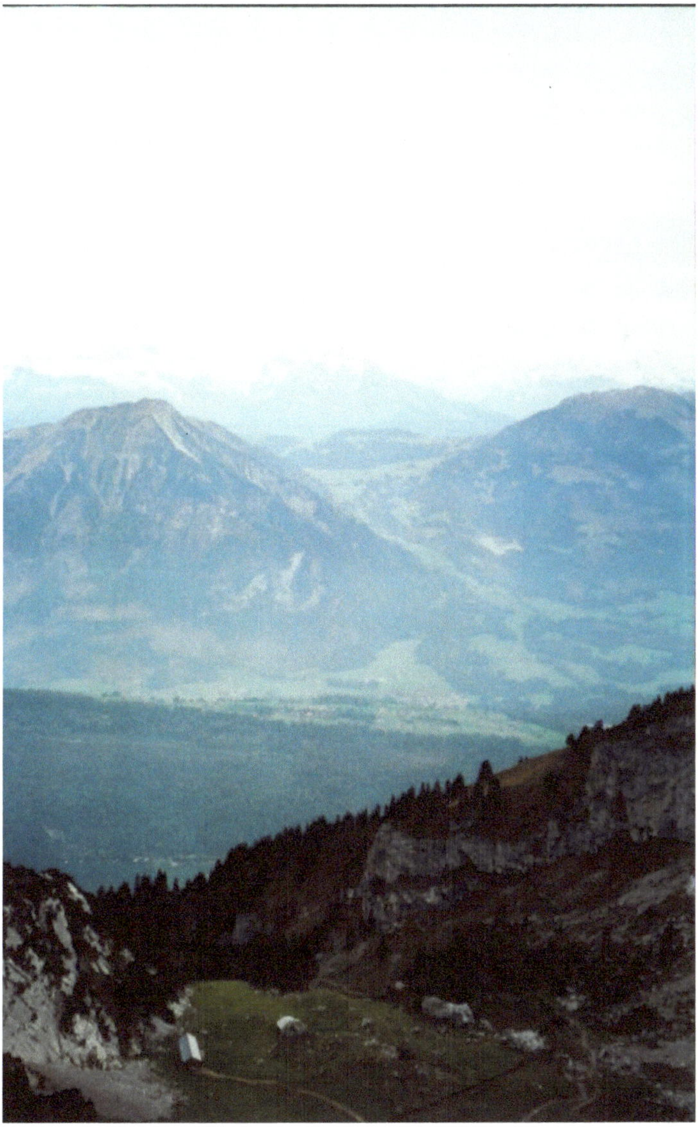

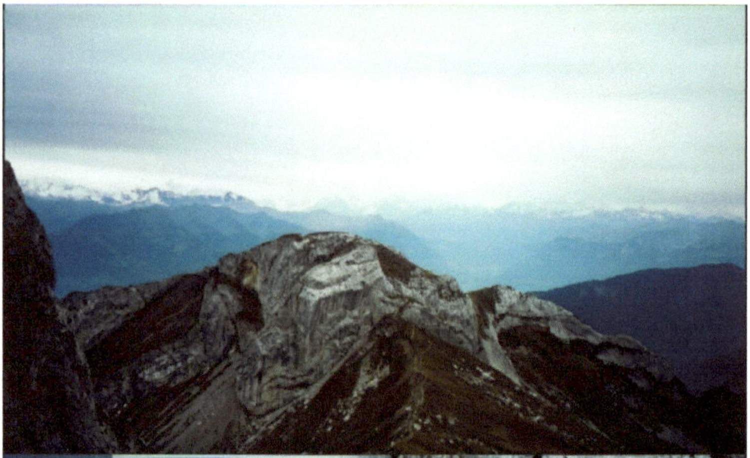

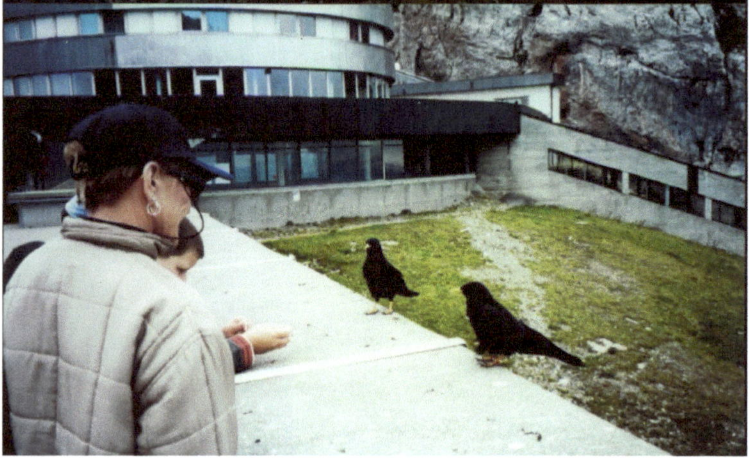

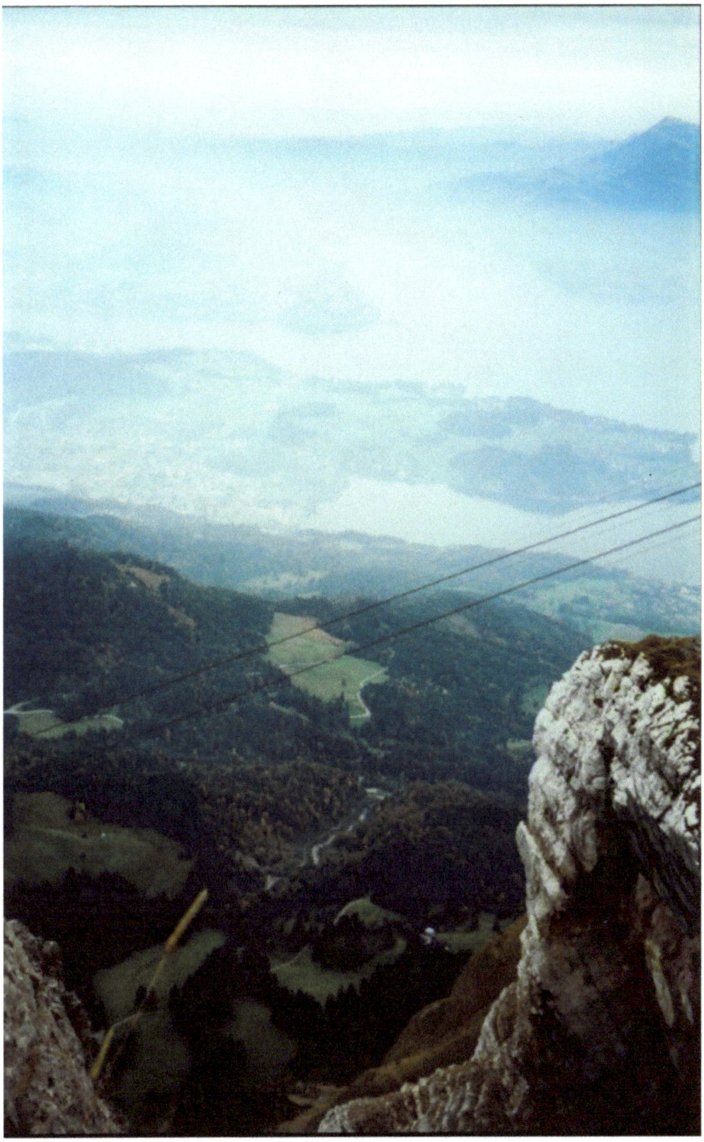

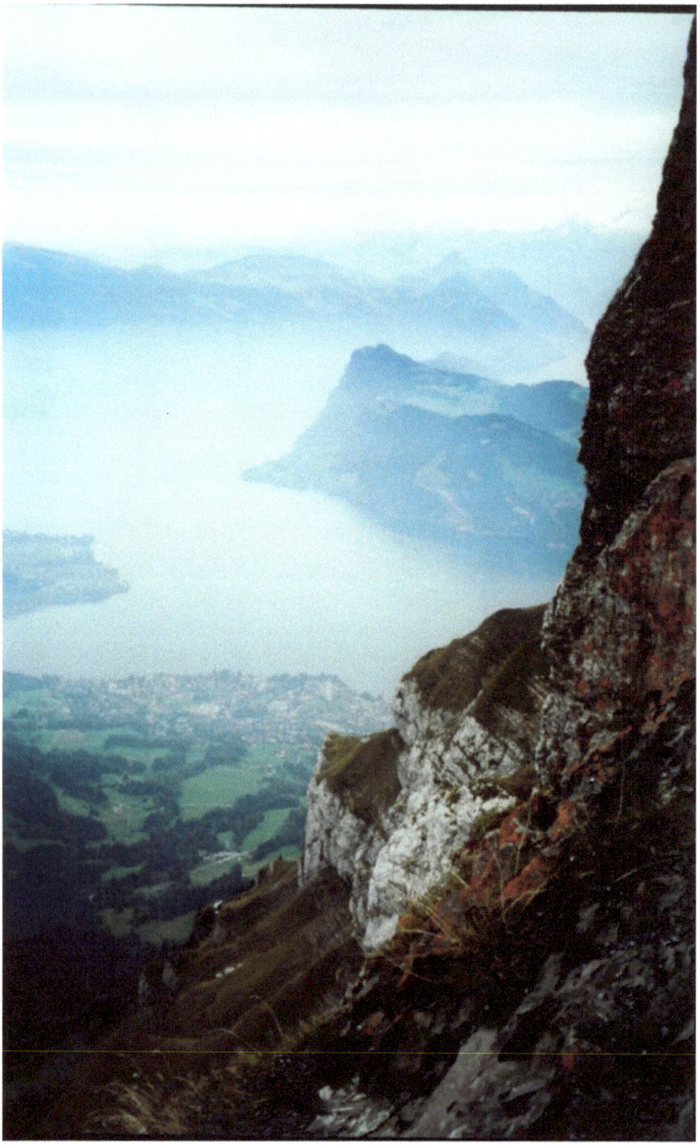

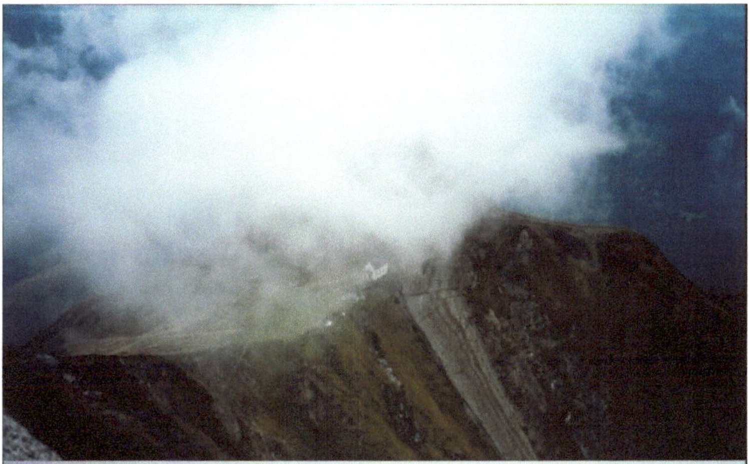
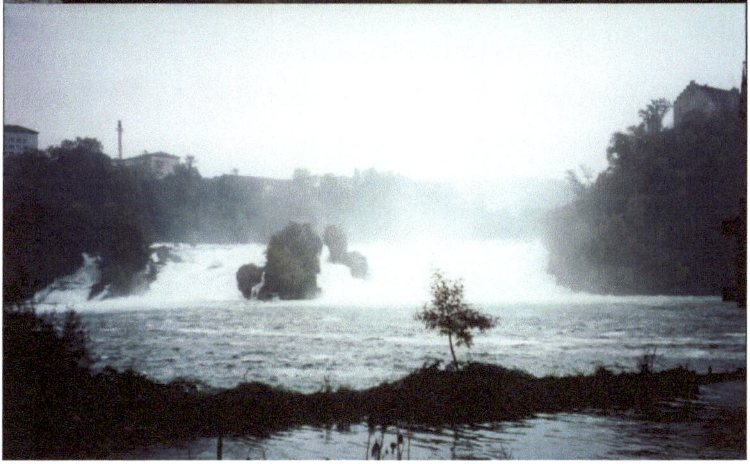

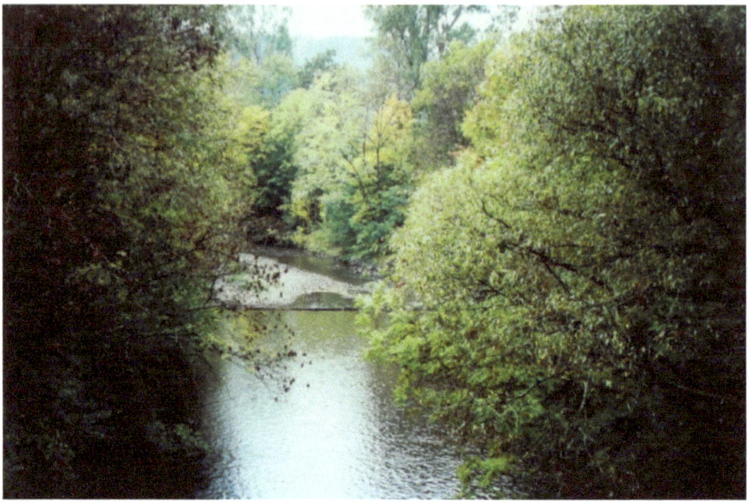

www.ingramcontent.com/pod-product-compliance
Lightning Source LLC
Chambersburg PA
CBHW040918180526
45159CB00002BA/521
* 9 7 8 1 5 1 4 6 1 8 5 8 5 *